What Color Are Tears?

A Grief And Loss Interactive Workbook
For Young Students

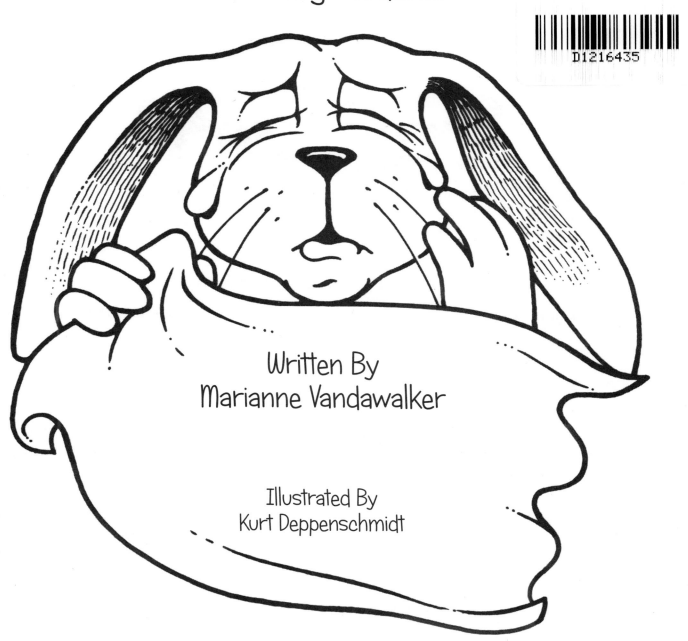

Written By
Marianne Vandawalker

Illustrated By
Kurt Deppenschmidt

Marianne Vandawalker

I am a retired counselor, but I continue to develop guidance activities that are successfully used in the classroom as well as in small-group and individual counseling settings. I actively keep up with new materials and emerging needs. My counseling experience succeeded 12 years as reading specialist and 28 years as a classroom teacher.

I've often found myself in need of good material to use in situations involving grieving and loss. Unbelievable as it still seems, a student died on our school's playground one Friday morning, and one of our kindergarten teachers died unexpectedly the following Monday morning. On those occasions, I conducted classroom guidance as well as small-group and individual counseling sessions. I wish I'd had *What Color Are Tears?* during those very trying times.

What Color Are Tears?

10-DIGIT ISBN: 1-57543-156-4   13-DIGIT ISBN: 978-1-57543-156-7

COPYRIGHT © 2008 MAR*CO PRODUCTS, INC
Published by mar*co products, inc.
1443 Old York Road
Warminster, PA 18974
1-800-448-2197
www.marcoproducts.com

PRINTED IN THE U.S.A.

Introduction

Counselors need a wide variety of materials in order to respond appropriately and effectively to a wide variety of situations and student needs. In the area of grief and loss, a counselor can never have too many resources. Material dealing with these sensitive topics must reach out to each child in a personal, realistically emotive way that encourages interaction and reaction. Students feel their emotions validated by feelings described in the story. Bibliotherapy helps readers relate to characters' predicaments and see how they resolve their situations and move on with their lives.

This story may be presented in a single session. Or individual pages may be presented in a workbook format as the youngsters show readiness.

The main character in *What Color Are Tears?* moves through the stages of grieving, and the positive way he deals with his loss are healing and instructive for students. Bitty Bunny is a likeable character, and Grandma Bunny lends a sense of nurturing and reassurance to a troubling situation.

Eliciting oral, written, or drawn responses to each question benefits the student by fixing solutions and answers in his or her developing mind.

How To Use *What Color Are Tears?*

PRE-READING PREPARATION:

Ask: Have you ever had a pet that died?
Have you ever had a family member or close friend who died?
What did you do when you found out about the death?
How did you feel about the loss?

VOCABULARY PREPARATION:

Memories: Do you have memories of something that happened to you?
What do you think memories are?

Tears: Have you ever cried or seen someone else's tears?
What causes tears?

Feelings: Tell me about different feelings that you have had.

3

Reading *What Color Are Tears?*

Say: I want to read you a story. Most of the pages include a question for you to think about and answer. When I get to a question, I will stop reading, and you may draw your answer or write your answer on the open space provided on that page. Some pages also include an additional question. After reading each of these questions, circle the bunny head that looks most like you feel. I will help you if you need help.

Begin reading the story aloud.

FINAL QUESTIONS:

1.   What part of this story do you remember most?
2.   Does something in this story remind you of something in your own life?
3.   What have you learned from this story?

FOLLOW-UP ACTIVITIES:

1.   Eat a favorite food that your special person enjoyed .
2.   Wear your special person's favorite color.
3.   Listen to your special person's favorite song.
4.   Use chalk to draw a sidewalk picture for your special person.
5.   Write a message for your special person. Put the message inside a balloon. Blow up the balloon, twist the tail to hold the air inside, and let the balloon and your message soar into the sky.

ASCA Standards

Standard A: Students will acquire the knowledge, attitudes and interpersonal skills to help them understand and respect self and others.

PS:A1   ACQUIRE SELF-KNOWLEDGE
PS:A1.1   Develop positive attitudes toward self as a unique and worthy person
PS:A1.4   Understand change is a part of growth
PS:A1.5   Identify and express feelings

Standard B: Students will make decisions, set goals and take necessary action to achieve goals.

PS:B1   SELF-KNOWLEDGE APPLICATION
PS:B1.4   Demonstrate effective coping skills for dealing with problems

Standard C: Students will understand safety and survival skills.

PS:C1   ACQUIRE PERSONAL SAFETY SKILLS
PS:C1.10   Learn techniques for managing stress and conflict
PS:C1.11   Learn coping skills for managing life events

What
Color
Are
Tears?

"Bitty Bunny, what makes your long ears and whiskers droop?" Granny Rabbit asks as she bustles about in the kitchen.

How do you look when you feel sad?

"I feel so sad since my friend Robbie Rabbit isn't here any more."

What makes you feel sad?

"You know, Bitty Bunny, drawing pictures of things you remember about your friend might help you feel less sad," Granny suggests.

"Granny's idea is a good one," Bitty Bunny says to himself, "but my memories are a sticky gray like a spider's web. No matter how hard I try, I can't sweep my mind clear enough to remember good things."

Is it hard for you to remember your special person?

"I want to draw pictures of my memories, but I'm having trouble choosing the colors. Right now, I want to draw with only the black crayon."

What color shows how you feel now?
Color the blank piece of paper on the table that color.

"What color are tears, anyway?" Bitty Bunny wants to know. "I think **blue** means **sadness**, and I wonder if tears are that color?"

Do you cry over the person you have lost?

"I can't make my tears stop. They run down my face like rain from a storm," sniffs Bitty Bunny.

How do you look when you cry?

"Tears sting my eyes like tiny pin pricks," Bitty Bunny says out loud. "I wish there were magic bandages to take my hurt away."

How do you feel about crying?

Granny tells Bitty Bunny, "It's all right to cry. Tears help wash the sadness away."

How do you feel after crying?

"I think about the smells from Robbie's burrow and from the pages of his favorite book," Bitty Bunny says. "In my mind, they seem white like snow."

What are some smells that connect
you to the person who has died?

"What color are smells?" Bitty Bunny wonders. "Smells don't stay with us. They fly away like little bits of fur blowing in the wind."

"I have so **many** feelings!" he tells Granny Bunny. "What color are feelings? I've seen pictures of hearts in science books, but my feelings are dark, like shadows in the late afternoon."

How do your feelings look since your special person has died?

16

"Maybe I can crawl into a deep hole and hide," thinks Bitty Bunny. "I can't believe Robbie's not here any more."

Where can you go to feel better?

17

Bitty Bunny's tears turns into sobs. His tears stream down his cheeks.

What can you do to make yourself feel better when you are sad?

"What color are sobs?" wonders Bitty Bunny. "Could sobs be the deep purple I see at night?"

Where on your body do you feel sobs?

Sometimes Bitty Bunny thinks he hears Robbie's voice. It moves in and out of the clouds around the moon. "What color are sounds?" Bitty Bunny wonders. "I guess the sounds I want to hear from Robbie Rabbit would be pale yellow, like the moon."

What sounds or words do you remember from your special person?

"Granny, sometimes I get so mad that I feel like screaming blood red." Bitty Bunny cries. "Robbie went into the woods by himself, and it's my fault he's gone!"

What do you do when you are angry?

Does what you do help you feel better?

"Just let the scream out," Granny says as she puts the muffins into the oven to bake. "Don't trap that anger inside yourself."

What is something else you could do when you are angry or blame yourself for something?

"I'm afraid to remember some things," Bitty Bunny admits. "What's the color of fear? Fear must be silver like steel, hard and cold like the ice on the pond."

What is one thing you are afraid of?

Bitty Bunny has fiery orange memories of times when he wasn't a good friend to Robbie.

What is one thing you wish you had never done to your special person?

What Color Are Tears? © 2008 Mar*co Products, Inc. 1.800.448.2197

"Try to remember the good memories," Granny says as she pats Bitty Bunny on the head.

What happy memory do you have of your special person?

"I wish memories could be soft green, like the weeping willow tree in our yard," Bitty Bunny tells Granny.

What helps you feel better when you feel sad?

"Use whatever color helps you feel better," Granny says as she checks the hot oven.

"I can't color any happy memories, because my happy colors are broken," Bitty Bunny cries. "I'll need a whole new box of crayons."

What is the hardest thing about things not being the way they were?

"Use your broken happy-colored crayons," Granny replies. "Even if the crayons are broken, each color can help you make pictures of your good memories."

What are your happy colors? Color each of the crayons one of your happy colors.

"I'll try," whispers Bitty Bunny. "Robbie always put a smile on my face. What color is happiness?"

What is one way your special person made you happy?

Color the ball the color of happiness.

"When I was with Robbie," Bitty Bunny says quietly, "I felt good, like my soft cotton tail feels good. He would laugh and joke and play tricks on me."

What are some things your special person did with you that made you feel good?

"Put those happenings in pictures," Granny encourages Bitty Bunny. "These drawings will be your memory pictures. Making them and looking at them later will help you remember good times you and Robbie had."

Would you like to create a collection of memory pictures?
Yes   No

"Granny is right," Bitty Bunny says as he tries to decide which colors to use. "Pictures began hopping into my mind right away, and they tell stories about Robbie and me.

"There's something else I can do, too. I can make a collection of Robbie's favorite things. I remember brown twigs, his cap, and the leaves on his bed."

What things do you have that remind you of your special person?

"But what will I do when I'm finished?" Bitty Bunny asks himself. "Will I have to put my collection of pictures and belongings in a box? Will I forget about them and the memories they show?"

Where would you keep your memory collections?

35

"Forget? No, you won't forget," Granny tells Bitty Bunny as she takes the carrot muffins out of the oven. "Your memories will be special keepsakes."

"This is going to be a lot of work," Bitty Bunny sighs. "It will take some time."

"Yes, it will. Working on something that's important to us almost always takes time and effort," Granny agrees as she spreads creamy yellow butter on a big, warm muffin for Bitty Bunny.

What else have you worked on that is important to you?

Bitty Bunny stops crying. His paws move quickly as he begins to draw his good memories of Robbie. The colors dance on the page as his memories march on, showing birthdays, games, races, and other fun times Bitty Bunny and Robbie had together.

Bitty Bunny smiles as he draws, colors, and remembers. With each drawing he makes, he looks back to a happy time he shared with Robbie. Each happy color he uses brightens his feelings and lightens his sorrow.

Bitty Bunny eats the big carrot muffin Granny has given him. The good taste makes him feel warm inside, and his tears dry. Now Bitty Bunny is sure that he understands what Robbie wants him to know.

39

Robbie's message to his friend is this:

Tears are not always

the same color.

As Bitty Bunny's good memories

heal his sadness,

his tears might even become invisible.

When that happens,

Bitty Bunny won't be able

to see his tears at all.